...tor: Virginia Lanigan
...ent Editor: Mary Ellen Lepionka
...Assistant: Nicole De Palma
...g Manager: Ellen Mann
...on Administrator: Elaine Ober
...Production Service: Schneck-DePippo Graphics
...signer: Deborah Schneck
...dministrator: Linda Knowles
...ition Buyer: Linda Cox
...cturing Buyer: Megan Cochran

Copyright © 1995 by Allyn & Bacon
A Simon & Schuster Company
Needham Heights, MA 02194

Library of Congress Cataloging-in-Publication Data

McNergney, Robert F.
    Foundations of education / Robert McNergney,
Joanne Herbert
        p.   cm.
    Includes bibliographical references and index.
    ISBN 0-205-13962-0
    1. Teaching—Vocational guidance—United States.
    2. Education—United States.   I. Herbert, Joanne.
    II. Title.
LB1775.2.M32   1995
371.1′002373—dc20   94-29562
                                                CIP

Printed in the United States of America
10 9 8 7 6 5 4 3 2 1   99 98 97 96 95 94

PHOTO CREDITS

Foundations of Educatio

THE CHALLENGE OF PROFESSIONAL PRACTICE

Robert F. McNergney
UNIVERSITY OF VIRGINIA

Joanne M. Herbert
UNIVERSITY OF VIRGINIA

Allyn and Bacon

Boston   London   Toronto   Sydney   Tokyo   Singapore